Be the Best You Can Be

KIRBY PUCKETT

As Told To Greg Brown

Illustrations by Tim Houle

Waldman House Press • Minneapolis

Text copyright © 1993 by Kirby Puckett and Greg Brown
Illustrations copyright © 1993 by Waldman House Press, Inc.

About Greg Brown: Sports have always played an important part in Brown's life, from the youth leagues
to earning All-Pac-10 honors in baseball at the University of Washington as an outfielder. He has been
a sportswriter the past 13 years, the last five at the Seattle Post-Intelligencer. Brown lives in Bothell,
Washington, with his wife and two children.

Waldman House Press, Inc. 525 North Third Street, Minneapolis, Minnesota 55401

Front cover photograph: Brian Peterson
Back cover photograph: Ken Levine, Allsport USA

Design by: MacLean & Tuminelly

The Major League Club insignias depicted in this product are trademarks
which are the exclusive property of the respective Major League Clubs and were
reproduced with the permission of Major League Baseball Properties and
may not be reproduced without written consent.

Library of Congress Catalog Card Number: 93-60188

ISBN 0-931674-20-4   First printing

My name is Kirby Puckett and I play center field for the Minnesota Twins.

Every time I go up to bat, I believe I am going to get a hit. Every time a ball is hit my way in the outfield, I believe I'm going to catch it. Every time I play in a game, I believe our team is going to win.

If you believe in yourself, you will succeed. Hey man, that's what it takes to be a winner and become the best you can be.

I was born in Chicago, Illinois, on March 14, 1961. My neighborhood was in one of the most dangerous ghettos on the south side of the city.

My mom and dad had nine children. I was the youngest. We didn't have much money even though my dad worked two jobs. We lived on the 14th floor of the apartments called the Robert Taylor Homes. A magazine once called the two-mile row of run-down buildings "the place where hope dies." But I never lost mine. You need hope to be the best you can be.

I never played Little League because we didn't have any ball fields around us. Only miles of concrete and streets. But I'm not ashamed of where I grew up. It doesn't matter where you come from. What matters is where you want to go, and how hard you work to get there.

I taught myself how to throw a baseball. I drew a chalk strike zone on a wall and had fun playing "strikeout" for hours. Sometimes my friends would come over to play baseball in my room with rolled up socks and a broom handle. Or we would play in the streets.

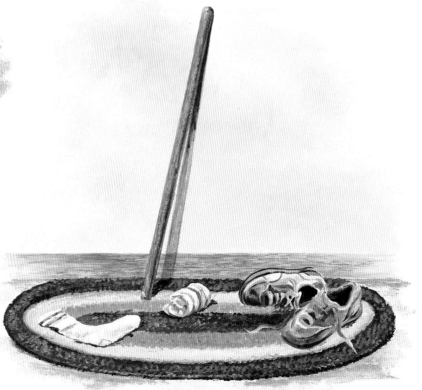

The first thing I ever won was a spelling bee in elementary school. I became a great speller because I brought home my spelling book and studied new words every single day. Over and over again. It wasn't always easy to practice so much, but I learned how good it made me feel when I did my best.

**What do you think
"Be the Best You Can Be" means?**

For one thing, it means you have to practice. A lot. If you go to a major league baseball game before it begins, you'll see players practicing their hitting and fielding. Even professionals need to practice to keep doing their best.

I earned a "B" grade average in school and I never did get in much trouble. But there were exceptions, like the time when I was in the fifth grade and my parents bought me a new suit for school pictures.

"I don't want you playing sports at school today," my mom said that morning. "Just stand on the side this one day."

"OK Mom, no problem," I said.

When recess came, all the kids played the tag game called "1-2-3 American Eagle." I watched for a while. I just couldn't take it.

I can play this one time, I thought. I'll be really, really careful. Sure enough, I tripped over someone's foot and tore a hole in the knee of my suit pants. Boy was I in trouble.

I went home thinking I could sneak upstairs to take off my pants so Mom wouldn't know. I walked in, covering the hole with my book, and there she was in the kitchen. I was caught.

"Hi Mom, how you doing?" I said as I gave her a kiss like always.

I couldn't fool my mother. She knew what I was up to.

"OK, move your book. Let me see what happened."

"What?"

"What are you hiding?"

"Nothing."

"Move the book," she said.

I was grounded for a whole month. I remember looking out the window and crying as I watched my friends play ball.

My friends said, "C'mon Kirby, can't you come outside? You can sneak out." "Nope," I said. "If I get caught, I'll be grounded longer."

If friends try to get you to do something you know is wrong like taking drugs, just say "Nope." I saw how drugs and alcohol can hurt people. I had to stop being with some kids because when you hang around troublemakers, trouble finds you. You can always meet new and better friends. I guarantee it.

When you feel pressured, just stand up for what you know is right. That's a part of being the best you can be.

In 1973, my family moved to a new neighborhood and I went to Calumet High School. It was the first chance I had to play on a real baseball field. I played third base and dreamed of being as good as Mike Schmidt and Brooks Robinson.

When I was 15, I played on a Chicago semi-pro summer team called the Pirates. In high school I had good seasons, but I didn't get any offers to play for a college or professional team.

After I graduated from high school, I went to work for a year at a Ford automobile factory. But my heart was set on succeeding as a baseball player, so the next summer I went to a Kansas City Royals tryout. I didn't make the Royals' team but Bradley University coach, Dewey Kalmer, spotted me there and offered me a scholarship.

Three weeks after I started school at Bradley, my dad died from heart problems. That was a terrible and painful time for me. When someone dies, it's out of your control completely. Even though I was always taught not to worry about things that were out of my hands, it was very difficult for me. I knew I had to go on with my life.

The best lesson my parents ever taught me was to be responsible because, as they said, they weren't always going to be around.

Everything seemed to go wrong then. Coach
Kalmer wouldn't let me play. All I got to do was
pinch-run. I was fast, 10 for 10 in stolen bases.

I got so frustrated that one day I went to my coach's office. "Why did you recruit me if you won't let me play?" I asked. He asked me if I could play anywhere else, like maybe center field.

"Sure I can," I said.

I had never played that position before, but I believed I could. So I became a center fielder. And that's where I've been ever since.

I was doing well at Bradley, but the next year I transferred to Triton Community College in River Grove, Illinois, to be closer to my mom. She was having a hard time dealing with my dad's death.

At Triton things really clicked for me. I was named the Region IV Junior College Player of the Year. I hit .472, stole 42 bases, and hit 16 home runs.

One thing many kids worry about is their size. Lucky for me, size doesn't matter much in baseball. Sure I'd love to be tall and slender like Darryl Strawberry of the Los Angeles Dodgers, but I'm not.

People come up to me all the time and say, "You look much shorter in person." I always say, "This is it. This is what I am." Being your best means to accept who you are and to make the most of what you have. To succeed you have to believe in the body and talents God gave you.

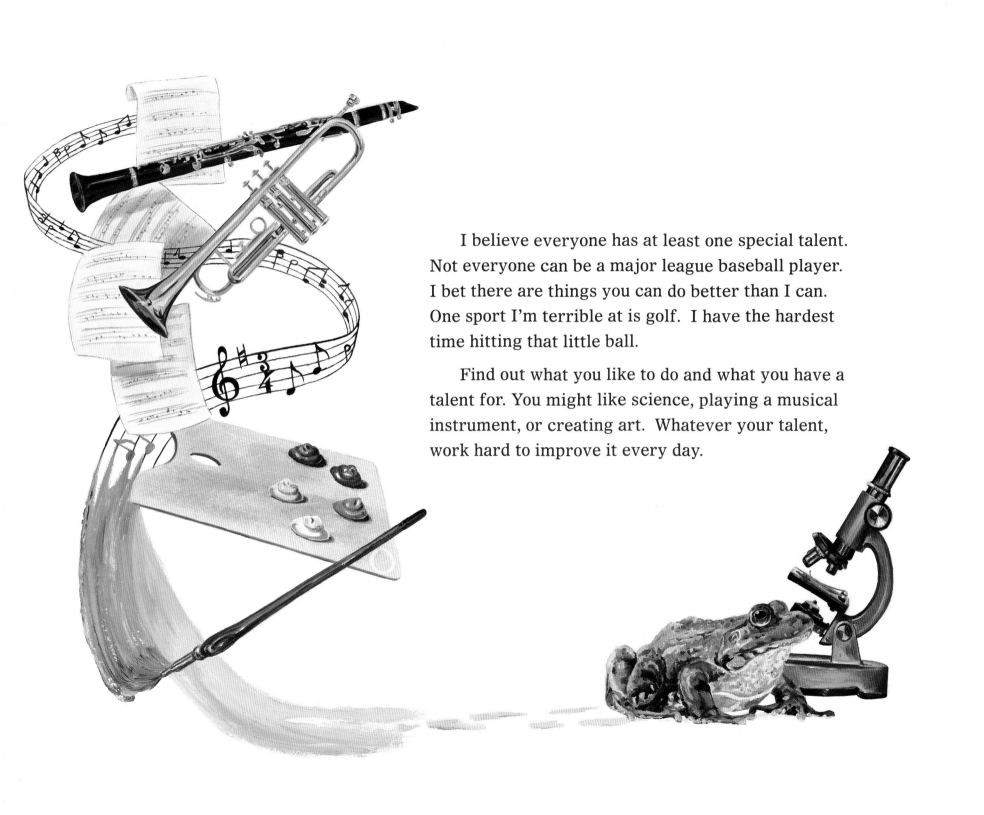

I believe everyone has at least one special talent. Not everyone can be a major league baseball player. I bet there are things you can do better than I can. One sport I'm terrible at is golf. I have the hardest time hitting that little ball.

Find out what you like to do and what you have a talent for. You might like science, playing a musical instrument, or creating art. Whatever your talent, work hard to improve it every day.

The Twins picked me in the first round of the January 1982 draft.

For a year and a half I played in the minor leagues. I did my best, and I was named Player of the Year, Best Batting Prospect, and Rookie of the Year.

Twins Draft Puckett

ANAHEIM

On May 8, 1984, I made my first major league appearance with the Twins in Anaheim, California. I was so broke that I had to borrow money for the taxi ride from the airport to the ballpark.

By the end of the game I had four hits. I had played my best. I became the ninth player in history to get four hits in my first major league game.

Being the best you can be also means you need to have confidence.
You've got to believe in yourself and never be a quitter. The first year
I played for the Twins, I didn't get a single home run. But I worked hard
and over the next two years I hit 35 home runs. I never quit believing
I could hit a home run.

In 1989, I was battling with Carney Lansford of the Oakland Athletics for the American League batting title. On the very last day of the season, I went 2 for 5 and won it with a .339 average. I felt like I was on cloud nine.

A week later my sister called me and said, "Mom is really sick." My wife and I got on a plane to Chicago but the plane was delayed. By the time we arrived, my mom had died.

I was devastated. I thought that it was the worst thing that had ever happened to me. If you have had someone die in your family, you know what I mean. I miss my mom and dad every day of my life. Sometimes being the best you can be means you have to keep moving forward even when you're hurting inside.

World Series 1991

WIDE WORLD PHOTOS

A Great Honor

On October 26, 1991, some people had given up hope that the Twins could win the World Series. We had won the first two games, but Atlanta had won the next three in a row. They needed just one more victory for the championship.

I hadn't done much in the first five games. I had just three hits in 18 tries for a low .167 batting average. I knew I could do better than that.

In batting practice before the sixth game I felt a surge of confidence. I said to the team, "You guys can jump on my back today. I'm going to carry us. I feel great today, man. We're going to win."

Finally, it was game time. More than 55,000 fans filled the Metrodome and waved their homer hankies to cheer us on. Millions of people all across the world watched on television. We stood on the foul line and listened to the singing of our National Anthem. I knew I would play my best.

In the third inning, the Braves had one out. Terry Pendleton was on first. Ron Gant was up to bat. Gant smacked the ball toward left-center field. I said, "That's not going over the wall. I can get it." I ran hard and timed my leap perfectly. I watched the ball until it fell into my glove. People call it "The Catch." The key was I never stopped believing I could catch that ball if I gave my best.

AT BAT	34	BALL	2	STRIKE	1	OUT	0

INNING	1	2	3	4	5	6	7	8	9	10	11	R	H	E
BRAVES	0	0	0	0	2	0	1	0	0	0	0	3	9	1
TWINS	2	0	0	0	1	0	0	0	0	0		3	8	0

Most baseball games last just nine innings, but we were tied 3-3 with the Braves so we had to play until one team won. By the bottom of the eleventh inning, the score was still 3-3. I was the first batter up.

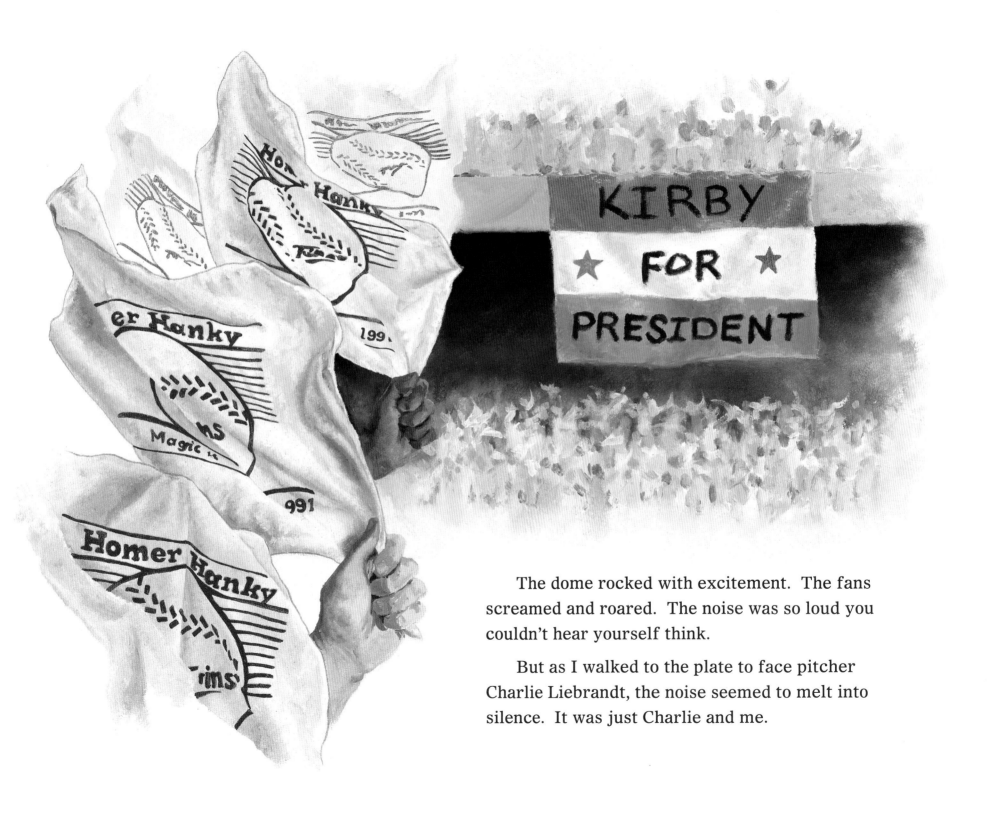

The dome rocked with excitement. The fans
screamed and roared. The noise was so loud you
couldn't hear yourself think.

But as I walked to the plate to face pitcher
Charlie Liebrandt, the noise seemed to melt into
silence. It was just Charlie and me.

"They've been throwing a lot of change-ups and getting you out," I told myself. "And don't swing at anything low."

That was a lot to ask. I usually swing at almost any pitch close to the strike zone. But I knew I could change and learn from my mistakes.

Sure enough, Charlie threw me a change-up low and away. I was tempted, but didn't swing. The umpire called it a strike. Two more fastballs made the count 2 and 1, two balls and one strike.

The fateful pitch was another change-up, only this one stayed up high in the strike zone. I took a good swing and watched the ball as it flew off my bat.

I didn't realize I had hit a home run until I rounded first base. Then I raised up my hands in celebration. Running the bases after that home run was one of the greatest thrills I've ever experienced.

"Yeessss. There is a tomorrow, there is a tomorrow," I kept telling myself. If we won one more game, we would win the World Series.

As I jumped on home plate to score the winning run, my teammates mobbed me. The fans yelled "Kir-by, Kir-by, Kir-by." That was a game I would never forget.

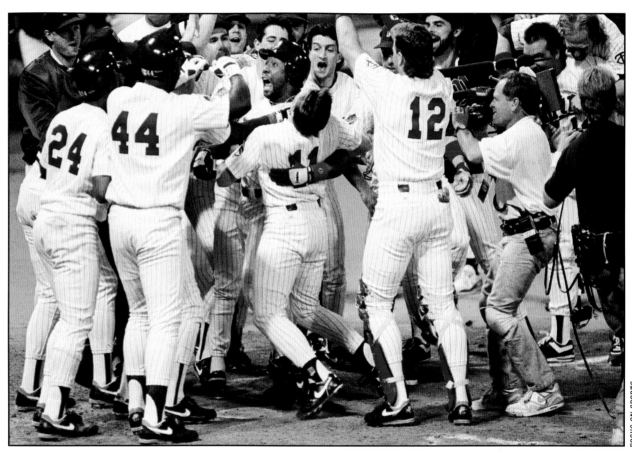

FOCUS ON SPORTS

Kir-by ... Kir-by ... Kir-by

After the game, I was told someone wanted to see me. "Is it the President, or some celebrity?" I thought. Instead, I met Joe Reis and his family next to the locker room. Joe had caught the home run ball I hit and wanted to give it to me. He said, "You are the only person who should have it."

KATHLEEN REIS

KATHLEEN REIS

I never could have imagined receiving such a generous gift. We took some pictures together and I autographed some things. I can't thank him enough. That ball is very special to me. Joe's genuine caring made me remember that there are so many good people in the world.

The next night we won the series title with a 1-0 victory. Jack Morris pitched the entire ten innings for the shutout.

When Gene Larkin singled in Dan Gladden for the winning run, we all went crazy. I jumped into Jack's arms and moments later got a kiss from my wife.

Then our whole team waved and thanked all of the Minnesota fans who believed in us, even though we had finished in last place the year before. We all knew that if we played the best we could, we would win.

It was the perfect way to end what many say will be remembered as the most exciting World Series in history.

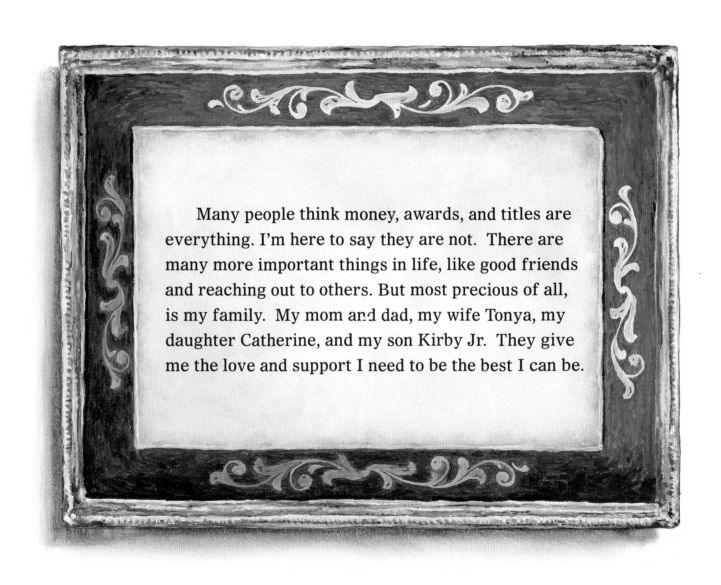

Many people think money, awards, and titles are everything. I'm here to say they are not. There are many more important things in life, like good friends and reaching out to others. But most precious of all, is my family. My mom and dad, my wife Tonya, my daughter Catherine, and my son Kirby Jr. They give me the love and support I need to be the best I can be.

Highlights

Selected by the Minnesota Twins in the first round of the January 1982 draft.

Made major league debut on May 8, 1984. Became ninth player in major league history to get four hits in first game.

Voted starting center fielder for the American League All-Star Team in 1986, the first of seven consecutive All-Star appearances dating to 1992.

Won American League batting title with .339 average in 1989.

Won Most Valuable Player award in 1991 American League Championship Series, hitting 9 for 21 with 2 home runs and 5 RBI in 5 games.

Two time World Champion with 1987 and 1991 Minnesota Twins.

On December 4, 1992 signed a five-year $30 million contract with the Minnesota Twins.

Be The Best You Can Be

Kirby Puckett #34

FOCUS ON SPORTS

Kirby's Extra Innings

Keep on Plugging
"I've never been a quitter. I always believed I could be the best I could be. To be your best you have to keep on plugging. That's why I work extra hard every single day . . . to try and stay a couple steps ahead . . . to stay sharp."

Help Others
"Try to help at least one person every day. Carry something for a friend, talk to someone who is lonely . . . or find your own special way to help. You'll feel good inside, I promise."

Treat People Right
"My parents taught me to always treat others how we want to be treated. Nobody wants things stolen from them, wants to get hurt or hear unkind words. So don't you do these things to others."

Remember to Have Fun
"Even when you work hard you can still have fun. I'm serious about my job, but I like to laugh and enjoy being around others."

Get an Education
"Go to school and be smart. If you're smart that's better than all the money in the world. There's a lot more to life than money . . . like the love of your family and friends."

Take it from Me
"Don't Smoke . . . Don't Even Start."

It's OK to Make Mistakes
"Don't worry about mistakes. Everyone makes mistakes. I once ran off the field and into the clubhouse thinking the game was over. It wasn't. I was supposed to bat, but nobody could find me so someone had to hit for me."

"Another time, I tripped while running off the field and I fell in front of about 50,000 fans in the Metro-dome. That was embarrassing."

Say Nope to Dope
"Some people think it's fun to use drugs like marijuana, crack, speed and alcohol. Drugs make you lose control of yourself. I always wanted to be in control, so I never used drugs. When friends asked me to try, I just said, "Nope." It's cool to be clean and in control."

Ya Gotta Believe
"To be good at anything you have to believe in yourself. It's easy when everything is going right. The hard part is believing in yourself when things go wrong. If I don't get a hit or if I make a mistake in the outfield I always believe I will do better next time."